Scotland & Northern Ireland Voices

Edited By Emily Wilson

First published in Great Britain in 2017 by:

Young Writers
Coltsfoot Drive
Peterborough
PE2 9BF
Telephone: 01733 890066
Website: www.youngwriters.co.uk

All Rights Reserved
Book Design by Ashley Janson
© Copyright Contributors 2017
SB ISBN 978-1-78820-886-4
Printed and bound in the UK by BookPrintingUK
Website: www.bookprintinguk.com
YB0315FZ

FOREWORD

Welcome to 'Once Upon A Dream – Scotland & Northern Ireland Voices'.

For Young Writers' latest poetry competition we invited pupils to write a poem inspired by their dreams. Poets could write about anything from their real-life aspirations and goals to a magical dream world they visit each night, a nightmare they have been trapped in or just an ideal place! We just wanted to see how creative you could be and to encourage you to express yourselves using your dreams as inspiration.

Of course they meant we received a great variety of poems about all sorts of different things which were great fun to read. Our poets were very imaginative with the content as well as the form and you are bound to find a poem to suit everyone in this collection.

The response we received from this competition was fantastic and it was great to see how inspired you all were with the topic! I would like to say a huge thank you to everyone who sent in a piece of work and well done to all the poets published in this collection. A special congratulations goes to *Cailín Traynor* for your wonderful poem which has been selected as the winner for this book. I hope you have all been inspired to carry on writing and that I see some more of your work in our future competitions!

Emily Wilson

CONTENTS

Winner:

Cailín Brigid Traynor (11) - St Brigid's Primary School, Newry	1

Independent Entries

Aseda Adusei (11)	2
Lucy Wilson	4
Juliette Wambergue (8)	5

Denamona Primary School, Omagh

Jayne Aimee Telford (10)	6
Lewis Mark William Henderson (9)	8
Paris McCrory (9)	10
Aaron Baxter (10)	12
Rachel Galbraith (9)	14
Leah Kee (9)	15
Levi Williams (10)	16
Valerie Patterson (9)	17
Rhys Hamilton (11)	18
Amanda Woods (8)	19
Katie Telford (10)	20
Lucy McCaul (8)	21
Jack Woods (8)	22
Adam Kee (9)	23
Isaac Michel Marechaux (11)	24
Jake Hamilton (10)	25

Dromore Primary School, Omagh

Lauren Bradley (9)	26
Amy Bradley (9)	27
Reece Edgar (9)	28
Amy Rutledge (10)	29
Chloe Crozier (8)	30

Drumahoe Primary School, Londonderry

Leah Caldwell (10)	31
Ben Brolly (10)	32
Tyler Gillespie (10)	33
Bobby Snodgrass (10)	34
Callum Crowe (9)	35
Callum Boyd (10)	36
Jodi Pollock (10)	37
Jay Curry (9)	38
Beth King (8)	39
Tristan Woolsey (9)	40
Lucy Leanne Simpson (8)	41
Emily Woods (8)	42
Madison Merchant (9)	43
Marcus Ramsey Bond (9)	44
Ellie-Leigh Magee (10)	45
Scott Laughlin (9)	46
Oliver Woods (9)	47
Lewis McLaughlin (9)	48
Ben Hunter (10)	49
Amy Edith Dunn (8)	50
Albert Boyd (8)	51
Kerry-Marie Campbell (10)	52
Ryan Peoples (10)	53
Oliver Allen (10)	54
John Hamilton (9)	55
Joel Cairns (9)	56

Duns Primary School, Duns

Christie Jones (10)	57

Gaelscoil An Chaistil, Ballycastle

Dearbhla Gairnéir (11)	58
Abbi McKinley (8)	59
Lucy Nic Conmara (10)	60
Isla Goodlad (10)	61
Aaron Mac Pháil (10)	62
Maebh Sands Robinson (9)	63
Aoife Kinney (9)	64
Críostpir ó Torráin (10)	65
Reannán Meggitt (11)	66
Aileen Goodlad (8)	67
Conán Mac Amhlaoibh (10)	68
Cónan Pearse Mac Fhirléighinn (9)	69

Malvern Primary School, Belfast

Macauley Mateer Carson (10)	70

Mullaglass Primary School, Newry

Jodie Sterritt (10)	71
Emily Annett (10)	72
Grace Hamilton (10)	74
Ellen Hamilton (10)	76
Emily Morrow (10)	77
Ruby Joanne McCartney (9)	78
Lois Boyd (10)	79
Nathan Cartmill (10)	80
Andrew McCartney (10)	81
Melanie Wylie (11)	82
Zara Moffett (10)	83
Rachel Paul (11)	84
Ellen Faloon (11)	85
Melissa Harshaw (11)	86
Yasmin Rose Muldrew (11)	87
Abbi Bradley (10)	88
Archie Alderdice (9)	89
Abbie Laura Nummy (11)	90

Newbuildings Primary School, Londonderry

Harley Muir (10)	91
Dylan Coyle (10)	92
David Guy (9)	93
Jason McIvor (9)	94
Samuel Wray (10)	95

Oakgrove Integrated Primary School, Londonderry

Caitlin-Lea Hamilton (10)	96
Ajala Tench (10)	97

Our Lady's & St Mochua's Primary School, Armagh

Meabh Quinn (10)	98
Dáire Finn (9)	100
Clare O'Hare (10)	101
Jessie Carr (10)	102
Sarah Renaghan (10)	103
Emma Gaffney (10)	104
Caoimhe Hourican (10)	105
Alejandro Arroita (10)	106
Caitlin Rafferty (10)	107
Aoife Drumm (10)	108
Orla Haughey (10)	109
Stephen Mone (10)	110
Emma Gollogly (9)	111
Seán óg McNaughton (10)	112
Shea Murray (10)	113
Shanna McDermott (9)	114
Niamh Duffy (10)	115

St Brigid's Primary School, Newry

Ellie Fagan (11)	116
Hollie McCann (11)	117
Amy McMahon (10)	118

St Colman's Primary School & All Saints' Nursery Unit, Banbridge

James Keenan (11)	119
Cormac McNally (11)	120
Clara Sheppard (10)	122
Líle McArdle (11)	123
Aoibheann Elizabeth Heenan (10)	124
Kyra Haughey (11)	125
Kate O'Rourke (11)	126
Killian Sean Loughlin (10)	127
Darragh Greenan (11)	128
Oisin McAvoy (11)	129
Paul Heenan (11)	130
Aaron McKay (11)	131
Carla Quinn (11)	132
Madison Greenan (11)	133
Ruairí McAvoy (11)	134
Aoife McArdle (11)	135

St Columba's Primary School, Kilrea

Niamh Orna Cunning (11)	136
Cághla Bradley (11)	138
Fearghal O'Kane (11)	140

St Patrick's Primary School Legamaddy, Downpatrick

Clodagh Burke (10)	141
John McLaughlin (11)	142
Ben Cope (11)	143

St Teresa's Primary School, Craigavon

Terri Devlin (10)	144
Aedan McGivern (9)	145
Emily Mulgrew (10)	146
Sophie-Rose Henderson (9)	147
Ben Whyte (10)	148
Martha Walsh (9)	149
Ella Forker (10)	150

Kieran Livingstone (10)	151
Amani Gallagher (10)	152

Torphichen Primary School, Bathgate

Georgia Rosenfeld (7)	153
Oskar de Joode (7)	154
Ewan Samper (7)	155
Laura Zoe Taylor (7)	156
Charlotte Conchie (7)	157
Rosie Kao (7)	158
Joe MacIver (7)	159
Tom McFarlane (7)	160
Cameron Fisher (7)	161
Merryn Binnie (7)	162
Nethuki Nuthara Perera (8)	163
Alexander Neave (7)	164
Fin Venters (7)	165

THE POEMS

The Very Berry Dream

I had a dream late last night,
I must admit it gave me a fright,
It wasn't about monsters or things that are scary,
It was about the baker Mary Berry,
I could see she was baking a very large bun.
I wanted to join in, it looked like lots of fun,
But when I went over to look at the cake,
I could see in the bowl there was a snake!
Mary mixed away and didn't think it was funny,
She said to me, 'Doesn't this look yummy?'
Just as she asked me to have a taste,
I ran away quickly without haste,
I woke up suddenly, glad to be awake,
There's one more thing, for sure I'll never ever bake!

Cailín Brigid Traynor (11)
St Brigid's Primary School, Newry

In Your Dreams...

Nonsense lurks inside my mind
And when I am asleep
Thoughts encircle round my brain
And into my head creep

Burgers waltz with unicorns
Dishes play with spoons
Forks prance around with knives
Which was sensible, I assumed
(Until I saw some knives
Stabbing innocent balloons!)

Crystal drops fall from the sky
And monkeys can speak!
Somehow I learn how to fly
And run through the week
(This may not make sense but confusion comes as we speak!)

I could simply say, 'It's Christmas!'
Then, 'Yay! Christmas has come!'
Or I could say it's Boxing Day
Then, 'Aww! Christmas is done!'
(Or I could say Christmas again and enjoy yet more fun!)

Then suddenly I wake up
My brother's jumping on the bed
I silently point to a note:
'Do Not Disturb' it said
(And couldn't he have kept to jumping on his own bed?)

Suddenly, the magic fades
I realise it's a dream
Then I wonder if my dreams
Are more meaningful than they seem
(And if they do, what do they mean?)

Aseda Adusei (11)

Dreamland

Once upon a dreamland
Up very, very high
The birds tweeting in demand
I want to eat some pie

The clouds are as fluffy as marshmallows
The sky is as blue as it can be
I'm sure I see an angel
And she's looking down on me

Fresh-cut grass is so green
Looks as good as mint ice cream
Flowers scattered like jelly tots
This is how life should be
Cuddles, kisses and candyfloss
This is the happy place for me.

Lucy Wilson

Midnight

M other kissed me goodnight and left the tent,
I ran outside to have some sneaky fun,
D id I know I was being watched?
N ow I find out it is a tiger!
I climb on her back and tell her of my life,
G reat to be friends with a tiger called Midnight.
H er nose touches mine and I turn into a tiger.
T ill I wake we are friends and I live with her.

Juliette Wambergue (8)

My Dreamy Dream

9 o'clock struck, time for bed,
I put my PJs on to sleep,
All snug I settle my head,
I fall asleep in a heap.

I wake up and see a chocolate river,
I spring from my bed to look around,
Holy smokes, I see my friends and Ariana Grande shiver,
Ariana said, 'Hello everyone. Don't make a sound.'

After a wee while I saw a lollipop,
And it looked very yummy,
I tasted it and it was a sugarpop!
When I put it in my mouth it tasted of gummy...

My friends, Ariana and I are walking down a path,
We see a massive hot chocolate cup,
We figured we are going to get a chocolate bath!
It explodes, but it all turns into milk!

We run away, oh so fast,
But it's flowing so fast we don't know what to do,
I thought today would be our last!
I have a brilliant idea that is new...

I see a lollipop tree that is very high,
I shout, 'Climb the lollipop tree!'
We climb up and up, we are safe near the sky,
I am so glad we are all safe and finally free.

Jayne Aimee Telford (10)
Denamona Primary School, Omagh

Candy Land

We were in a rocket
Going to the moon
But something loosened a socket
It looked like I was in a cartoon.

The people of Candy Land
Were actually quite friendly
They helped us to our feet and
They were extremely smelly.

I saw a house of toxic waste
The sour mark was red!
I licked and I tasted a sour taste
I thought I would be dead!

I heard an egg hatching
It was a dragon's egg
His wings started flapping.
Oh no! The shell was stuck to his leg.

The dragon prepares for attack
He aims for my face...
And *smack!*
He hits in the right place.

I grabbed my blade
And yelled 'En garde.'
'Well, well,' he said
And kicked me back a yard.

A marshmallow monster appears
He has smelly feet
He holds giant spears
Which scare the birds that tweet-tweet.

I killed the monster!
I had victory!
We each had a giant oyster
In a dwelling tree.

Lewis Mark William Henderson (9)
Denamona Primary School, Omagh

Tarantula

I see some meteorites in the sky,
Some people think they will fly!
Suddenly, I'm in a different galaxy,
And then I think it is a lie!

But then I figure something out,
Earth's not here, it's not about.
I did not know that there is no snow,
Then I feel a big, big blow!

Suddenly, spiders come out of a house,
One of them bites me, oh! And there's a mouse.
I suddenly faint, I have a dream,
I know these planets, I seem to need to scream.

I'm suddenly able to fly,
I think I will drop and die!
I fly up high,
Into the sky.
I land on the ground,
With a massive pound!

As soon as I land,
I hear a noisy band.
I turn into a huge spider,
Then I see a horse rider!

Whoever's reading this now would probably get
a fright,
Now that I'm awake I see a bright light.
And now that I'm finished I don't know what to say...
But it's nice when your imagination runs away!

Paris McCrory (9)
Denamona Primary School, Omagh

The Bear

I woke up in the night,
As I heard a loud noise, oh so loud,
It gave me such a fright,
My bed started to float like a cloud.

I heard the noise again,
I jumped out of my bed,
It then started to rain,
The noise stayed in my head.

I ran down the hall,
To see what was the matter,
On the back of my neck I could feel something fall,
In the living room there was such a clatter.

There was a big bear with razor-sharp teeth,
I went to the kitchen and got a pan,
He looked like a thief,
I said this will ruin your plan.

My dad was nearly in tears,
My mum came down the stairs,
Boy, was she full of fear,
Everybody really did care.

I woke up from my dream and ran down the stairs,
I walked round and round,
There is nobody here,
On my face there is definitely a frown!

Aaron Baxter (10)
Denamona Primary School, Omagh

The Man

Me and my friends,
Stick together in the end!
When the man in the red suit comes we struggle to cope,
We stay together and pray and hope!

We turn around and see these eyes,
Oh we hope the devil is a disguise.
Click goes the door, we run to tell Mum,
Oh no! We see the man, he tells us to come!
We all scream and then run!

What has happened?
I have woken up in my cosy bed,
Oh I really do have a sore head.
Click, clomp, click, what's that?
I do hope it's just the cat.

I pinch myself to see if I'm awake,
I can now smell a delicious cake!
I realise it's actually my birthday...
And those awful thoughts were just a nightmare!

Rachel Galbraith (9)
Denamona Primary School, Omagh

Holiday Dreams

First on Saturday morning we woke up late,
We packed up very fast, some may say it's great.
Because we woke up late Adam's family had already left.
Adam and Nicole have got a new kitten called Beneft.

The next day we worked hard to unpack,
We put all the things on the rack.
On Monday we went to Barries,
We then went to eat out at Darries.

We met two dogs called Brewfis and Molly,
Everyone thought they were very jolly.
Can we take them home?
Yes, we can take them home now.

I am cuddled up with Brewfis the dog,
What's that I see, is it fog?
Oh no! It's all been a dream. *Boom!*
Everything's gone now. I feel doom!

Leah Kee (9)
Denamona Primary School, Omagh

Builder

Dig, dig, dig goes the digger.
The bucket lifts the stones, bang!
The hole gets bigger and bigger.
The hole gets bigger and bigger.
Oh! The phone has now rung.

Oh! The bricks have fallen down.
They can't keep on building at all.
I bet that man feels like a clown.
Oh no! More bricks start to fall.

The battery goes flat.
They run out of cement.
There's now a big rat.
They all sit scared in a tent!

What a mess!
No work is done.
They will have to confess.
Or go for a big run.

I wake up, my mum comes in.
Was it a dream?
I did hear that din.
It was definitely a strange, strange dream.

Levi Williams (10)
Denamona Primary School, Omagh

The Super Cousins

Saturday night, very late,
I need a drink with my mate.
Oh, I have such a fright,
The kitchen is such a sight.

Now again in the bed I'll go to sleep,
Then my head starts to hear a *beep, beep*...
I feel the heat from the blanket around me,
But the mess I can still see.

Now I need to find the beep,
But Ellie-Mae isn't asleep.
I found the beep, it's our clocks.
It's now muffled with our socks.

The fairies give us superpowers, I become Ice Girl,
Ellie-Mae became a fairy and did a whirl.
We defeated some villains on roofs,
Ellie-Mae said, 'Nice moves!'

Valerie Patterson (9)
Denamona Primary School, Omagh

The Abandoned Hut

I find myself in a hut with a lot of loot.
On the other side of the world.
There is a severed foot.
And randomly, my hair is curled.

I see a random dancer.
And two spiders staring at me.
The dancer kept shouting, 'Prancer!'
The spiders were scary, so I want to flee.

I'm now with a flying builder in the sky.
And a friendly clown.
I look down and we are so high.
On the funny clown's face there is now a frown.

In the hut I find a hidden door.
Guarding the exit there are two monster guards.
The hidden door is camouflage on the floor.
The guards chase us for yards.

Rhys Hamilton (11)
Denamona Primary School, Omagh

A Day In Death Land

I'm walking in the forest in the afternoon.
I see something in the sky, I think it is the moon.
I hear a rustle in the bushes, its a clown.
Ohh... so I run back to the small town.

It is dinner time and I'm having chicken pie.
My sister didn't eat her dinner and so told a lie.
Then Lyndsay and I go outside and see a guy.
We rush inside and shout goodbye!

I hear a noise and I'm scared.
I run away and fall, a big purple thing stares.
I run down the tunnel and trip.
And when I trip I do a big flip!

Flash! Bang! I scream, 'Yay! It was all a bad dream!'

Amanda Woods (8)
Denamona Primary School, Omagh

Sleepover

It was Friday at 10pm when we went to bed.
We ate some Jelly Babies.
And chatted about that boy Fred.
We slept like smelly babies.

We went to Asda
And ran down the isles
We bought some pasta
And drove for miles.

Jordana and I saw some cars
They drove so fast!
We saw some yellow stars.
They flew quickly past!

Back in my room
There was a fat pig
It was holding a broom
And wearing a wig.

Suddenly... we wake up and it was all a dream!
There were no cars or stars
The big fat pig wasn't real
I think I might have been to Mars!

Katie Telford (10)
Denamona Primary School, Omagh

Football Fever

I had a dream where I arrived at a pitch.
We went inside and I met someone rich.
There were people doing a fancy jig.
My eyes started to grow wide and big!

There was a bright flash.
Where Laucs and Firmino came out like a dash.
They took me to Melwood!
I started calling them dudes.

Well, I started to feel bad.
And I felt hungry and sad.
So, Daddy and I got a Subway.
I did it the club-way.

When I got back I started to play football.
With such a cute ball!
It had the symbol 'Nike' on it
And yes I've got the kit!

Lucy McCaul (8)
Denamona Primary School, Omagh

Me In Candy Land

It's 8.30pm and it's time for bed.
I brush my teeth and get a sore head.
I get into bed and fall asleep.
Then I hear a banana bus beep.

The banana bus takes me on a journey.
We arrive in Candy Land in a hurry.
I see the king's castle burning, I get there in a flash.
As soon as I get there it's covered in ash.

The king comes out shouting.
'What's this all about?'
Boom, bang, pop, crash!
I'm in my bed sleeping and it's all over in a flash!

Jack Woods (8)
Denamona Primary School, Omagh

The War Of The Kingdoms

I live in Asguard.
I am a guard.
My name is Ridge.
I guard the rainbow bridge.

Loki sent his snow giant.
He says he is reliant.
The fire soldiers defeat the monster.
Loki says he will now get a monster.

I must defeat him!
If I hit him on the eye,
He will cry and die.
Then I wake up bright.
Because I have had an awful fight!

Adam Kee (9)
Denamona Primary School, Omagh

The Football Match

Out of the taxi I jump,
I run to the pitch in a flash,
Into a person I bump,
Oh no, what a crash!

The match begins as the whistle blows, wow!
What a joy to watch a football match,
Everyone starts to cheer and gloat.

I feel a bump,
I wake up and scream, this has made me jump,
It was all a dream.

Isaac Michel Marechaux (11)
Denamona Primary School, Omagh

Barcelona Dream

I'm in the Barcelona team.
Messi shows me how to shoot.
I see a hot, hot puff of steam.
It takes a funny root.

I awake, there's no team.
Oh no! It's all been a dream.
One day it will all be so real.
It won't be just what I feel.

Jake Hamilton (10)
Denamona Primary School, Omagh

Dreamland

Once I was floating in Dreamland
Surrounded by fluffy white clouds
I did not know where I was at first
And then I suddenly found...

Fairies dancing all around me
Fluttering their beautiful wings
Talking with shrill high voices
Trying to take everything in.

Unicorns appeared out of nowhere
Flying as quick as lightning
Letting me have an exciting ride
Reminding me of a wonderful time.

When I was floating in Dreamland
Surrounded by fluffy white clouds
I met the fairies and unicorns
Then something woke me up; very loud!

Lauren Bradley (9)
Dromore Primary School, Omagh

The Land Of Dreams

The land of dreams
Is full of magic
It's very, very busy
It's getting ready for tonight.

Fairies are carrying potions
I can hear them talking away
They look very, very busy
They are waiting for tonight to begin.

The unicorns are waiting for something
I'm not exactly sure what it is
I'm sure it's really exciting
I'm waiting for it all to begin.

Amy Bradley (9)
Dromore Primary School, Omagh

Under The Sea

U nder the sea is amazing
N ow it's time to go on a trip
D own on the seabed
E ast we travel with seaweed in our way
R ight we go next with lots of colourful fish

T he adventure is almost over, we
H ead to the city called
E lephant

S oon it is time to go
E ast and right back
A ahhh! Oh, it was only a dream!

Reece Edgar (9)
Dromore Primary School, Omagh

Magic Land

Once upon a dream
I saw a unicorn and fairies
What a beautiful scene
A cottage built with colourful wafers
And roses around the door

Fabulous flowers and plants scattered around
Smiling happily in the sun
Petals on the ground
By the cottage door

Once upon a dream
Wishing to stay there forever and ever
Magical place full of happiness
Awakened with an owl's scream!

Amy Rutledge (10)
Dromore Primary School, Omagh

The Pirate Dream

P irates lived long ago
I see one in my dream
R edbeard flashes in my eyes
A ll the pirates trying to take the treasure
T o a secret place
E veryone chasing
S o scary!

Chloe Crozier (8)
Dromore Primary School, Omagh

Anna Doll

A nna is a warm-hearted doll, when her owners are watching
N ight is now, everyone's sleeping and the children's door key she's unhooking
N ow she loads her gun
A s she stands there staring at me I'm shaking like a leaf in a very windy breeze, then she said, 'Farewell hun.'

D ented and unloved, Anna wants revenge
O wned by a doll wrecker, well that's what happened to Anna but revenge is a challenge
L onely Anna pulls out her gun and pulls on the trigger
'L oser,' she shouts as bullets and her grin were getting bigger.

Leah Caldwell (10)
Drumahoe Primary School, Londonderry

Clown Killer

C reepy killer at the end of my bed going to stab me at the end
L aughing with knife in hand, I cannot describe my fear
O range mask, my face turned as purple as a pen
W orried so much, I woke up in bed
N ever did I go to a circus again

K iller not here, it was my desolate fear
I was sacred half to death
L aughing to myself I knew it wasn't real
L iterally I saw an illusion, it gave me lots of confusion
E ither way I am going mad, I can hear the killer's laugh
R ight I heard a knock at the door, wait, it is only four.

Ben Brolly (10)
Drumahoe Primary School, Londonderry

Killer Clown

K iller clowns are here because Halloween's here
I 'm full of fright, Halloween is here
L oving trick or treating, oh, what a particular feeling
L iking being watched
E veryone's running scared
R attling noises from an alley so dark and scary

C ool and chilly on Halloween night
L ight and bright, you might get a fright
O h no, we see a clown, I wonder why he's got a frown
W ooh, I'm surprised he is slow
N ow I'm quite scared, he's picked up the pace, we got away, now we're safe.

Tyler Gillespie (10)
Drumahoe Primary School, Londonderry

Unknown Clown

U p in the city of Bukentums
N ight is when clown monsters come out
K now I live in Bukentums
N ever people thinking it's going to stop, not even a doubt
O utside in the darkness they feast on blood
W hat do I do?
N ow I see one outside and it slipped on the mud

C an it get in?
L isten and hear because I hear the door opening!
O h no, I'm telling God to forgive my sin
W hat do I do, he is running
N ow I see him he's got a knife.

Bobby Snodgrass (10)
Drumahoe Primary School, Londonderry

My Bed Is Like A Racing Car

My bed is like a racing car
When I'm tucked in, I travel far
I leave behind my family and pets
And travel to places, as if I have jets

I drive past corn waving in the fields
And when I stop, I read my favourite fairytales
Then I drive by the shore and I see the sea
After that, it's home for tea

I blink my eyes in the morning light
My car is home, I can't wait until tomorrow night
Me and my car go cruising in my dreams
The morning comes soon, or so it seems.

Callum Crowe (9)
Drumahoe Primary School, Londonderry

Killer Turtle

K iller turtle, scary as could be
I n hope to see
L ovely amounts of blood gushing from your skull
L oving blood is what he calls not dull
E ventually, at you doorstep
R ight then, go do a quick prep

T orture is what they seek
U nwelcoming smile he greets
R un child, run like a bolt
T he others are coming to roll your skin in salt
L eave! Maybe grab a poll
E ventually, they will catch up and eat your soul!

Callum Boyd (10)
Drumahoe Primary School, Londonderry

Diamonds And Jewels

D iamonds are so shiny like gold
I nside the cave I see the dwarf hitting the wall to find diamonds
A bold, beautiful, glittery diamond I see at the bottom of the hall
M aybe they could end up in a mall?
O n my trip I went on a plane, it was very fast
N ow I am here I better make the most of it and have as much fun as possible
D own the hall we go, I was about to fall off the cliff
S uddenly, there are no more jewels or diamonds shining in front of me.

Jodi Pollock (10)
Drumahoe Primary School, Londonderry

Mr Mimulus

M r Mimulus is on the loose
R uns like a moose

M y heart is pounding, I hear footsteps nearby
I feel the door opening on my arm, I know I must be sly
M r Mimulus pulls out his knife, my death must be near
U ntil I wake up my life is saved, Mr Mimulus said, 'Oh dear.'
L ife would've returned to normal but I saw my near killer again
U nless my dream is coming true, then I must...
S trive... for... my... life!

Jay Curry (9)
Drumahoe Primary School, Londonderry

My Bed Is Like A Racing Car

My bed is like a racing car
When I'm tucked in, I travel far
I leave behind my pet dog Poppy
And drive to places that make me soppy

I drive past my favourite chippy
In the winter the road is slippy
I watch the sunrise, it makes me glad
And then I see my mum and dad.

I blink my eyes, I was dreaming
I'm back home, my alarm is screaming
My car goes cruising every night
And drives home in the morning light.

Beth King (8)
Drumahoe Primary School, Londonderry

My Bed Is Like A Rocket Ship

My bed is like a rocket ship
When I'm tucked in I take a trip
I leave behind the Earth below
And blast off, into space I go.

I whizz past planets and the stars
Up past Jupiter, then past Mars
I see a flying saucer race past
Travelling to Earth, going so fast.

I open my eyes, I'm back in my room
I'm in my bed, not on the Moon
Tomorrow I might zoom back to space
To visit more aliens and have a race.

Tristan Woolsey (9)
Drumahoe Primary School, Londonderry

My Bed Is Like A Feather Nest

My bed is like a feather nest
When I'm tucked in, I take a rest
I leave behind my busy school
I fly to places very cool.

I fly past towns and houses tall
With fast wings I can touch them all
I watch the stars twinkle in the sky
And then I see my bed close by.

I blink my eyes, I'm in my room
My wings are home, I'll sleep soon
My wings go cruising every night
And fly home in the morning light.

Lucy Leanne Simpson (8)
Drumahoe Primary School, Londonderry

My Bed Is Like A Frozen Castle

My bed is like a frozen castle
When I get out, it is a big hassle
I leave behind my neighbour's dog
And drive to places with lots of fog.

I drive past trees with many green
With many people that are very mean
I watch the sunset going down
And then I have a big frown.

I blink my eyes and see my puppy
And then I remember he is very mucky
My car goes racing every night
And drives home in the morning light.

Emily Woods (8)
Drumahoe Primary School, Londonderry

My Bed Is Like A Racing Car

My bed is like a racing car
When I'm tucked in, I travel far
I leave behind my busy day
And drive to places like boutiques.

I drive past lots of fashion shops
That sell a lot of pretty tops
I watch the people stare and glare
And then I see my hair turning fair!

I blink my eyes, I open them slowly
My car is home and I am holy
My car goes cruising every night
And drives me home in the moonlight.

Madison Merchant (9)
Drumahoe Primary School, Londonderry

Footballer

F ight to get in the first team
O pening game of the season
O ut to win the game
T he ref though already blew the whistle for whatever reason
B ig names to look out for this season
A ll the pressure is on us
L earn to reach success
L ive your dream
E ntire world is watching us
R ival everyone
S uddenly I woke up, so I dream for a few more years to be one.

Marcus Ramsey Bond (9)
Drumahoe Primary School, Londonderry

My Bed Is Like A Racing Car

My bed is like a racing car,
When I'm tucked in, I travel far.
I leave behind my pet mouse,
And travel to a place with a house.

I drive past a forest with logs,
And decided where I'm going to walk my dogs.
And watch the sunlight upon the night,
And then I see my night light.

I blink my tired, sleepy eyes,
Could they be telling me lies.
I wake up to see my racing car, it's outside.

Ellie-Leigh Magee (10)
Drumahoe Primary School, Londonderry

Footballer

F ighting through the match trying to win
O ff and on the footballers come
O pening up the pitch the crowd come in
T he players get into position, well some
B alls being kicked through the air
A round the stadium the players run
L egging it without a care
L oudly bangs the sound of a gun
E veryone falls to the floor with fear
R un everyone, run, the killer is near.

Scott Laughlin (9)
Drumahoe Primary School, Londonderry

My Bed Is Like A Motorbike

My bed is like a motorbike
When I'm tucked in, I go for a hike
I leave behind my Christmas bell
And go to places that have wells

I drive past fields of corn
And find the place I was born
I look at the boar
And then I see my bedroom door

I blink my eyes and stretch out wide
My car is now in the drive
My car goes cruising every night
And drives home in the morning light.

Oliver Woods (9)
Drumahoe Primary School, Londonderry

My Bed Is Like A Racing Car

My bed is like a racing car
When I'm tucked in, I travel far.
I leave behind my worries
And drive to places that serves nice curries.

I drive past cool places
With people that have funny faces.
I watch the sun
And then I see my mum!

I blink my eyes, I see a kite
My car is home, I feel alright.
My car goes cruising every night
And drives home in the morning light.

Lewis McLaughlin (9)
Drumahoe Primary School, Londonderry

My Bed Is Like A Racing Car

My bed is like a racing car
When I'm tucked in, I travel far
I leave behind Benone
And drive to places unknown.

I drive past fields of green
With animals I've never seen
I watch the stars and moon
And then I see my room!

I blink my eyes, I wiggle my toes
My car is home and nobody knows
My car goes cruising every night
And drives home in the morning light.

Ben Hunter (10)
Drumahoe Primary School, Londonderry

My Bed Is Like A Racing Car

My bed is like a racing car
When I'm tucked in, I travel far
I leave behind the crazy day
And drive to places I can stay

I drive past trees
And then I fall on my knees
I watch the sunset go
Then I see the river flow

I blink my eyes, I stretch out wide
My car is home, right outside
My car goes cruising every night
And arrives home in the morning light.

Amy Edith Dunn (8)
Drumahoe Primary School, Londonderry

My Bed Is Like A Racing Car

My bed is like a racing car
When I'm tucked in I travel far
I leave behind my dog Mark
And drive to places that are dark
I drive past where I was born
With my bear as we go on
I watch the man slam the door
And then I see my mother
I blink my eyes, I stretch my legs
My car is home as I eat eggs
My car goes cruising every night
And drives home in the morning light.

Albert Boyd (8)
Drumahoe Primary School, Londonderry

Prisoner

P risoner Pete is stealing sweets
R ound the corner of the street
I s he stealing more sweets to eat?
S ounds like munching and crunching every sweet
O n the ground I hear his feet
N ever ever will Prisoner Pete eat real food but sweets
E ating all the sweets, why oh why Prisoner Pete?
R ight or left, no one can tell what way he went!

Kerry-Marie Campbell (10)
Drumahoe Primary School, Londonderry

Wizard

W hen I find myself in a new land
 I start to hear a sound, it's a
Z *zzzzzeeeerrtt*, a wizard house
A wizard saw me, another sound, *peeerfttt*
R unning, the wizard came faster and faster
D ashing to me, he gave me a drink, he said, 'Drink it.'
   I did. I went as blue as a pen, but I woke up in my bed.

Ryan Peoples (10)
Drumahoe Primary School, Londonderry

Monster

M idnight fell, I woke up then
O n that dreadful scary night
N ot much later I saw a thing with a very long knife
S o it killed Bobby and grabbed me tight
T ill my mum stabbed me with a knife
E very time I think of it I get very scared
R elieved I won't have another scary day.

Oliver Allen (10)
Drumahoe Primary School, Londonderry

My Bed Is Like A Dragon

My bed is like a dragon
When I'm tucked in, I'm like a bun
I leave behind my books
And ride to places off the hook
I ride past bends
With a few hens
I watch the trees blowing in the breeze
And then I see my light so bright
I blink my eyes, I get such a fright
And then I see my favourite kite.

John Hamilton (9)
Drumahoe Primary School, Londonderry

Monster

'M onster!' I yell
 O ver and over again
 N ot a way to Hell
 S nake-like it looks
 T errifying it is
 E rgo it is not like a hat
 R acing and racing I am.

Joel Cairns (9)
Drumahoe Primary School, Londonderry

Mythical Miles

Meandering down the magical path,
Magnificent, colourful, glowing trees,
My mind clearing of all my wrath,
I hear the buzzing sound of bees.

I saw two paths, I had to choose one,
Left was the way I decided to go,
In the dark sky there was no sun,
I walk terrified, a little too slow.

I heard a rustle in the wood,
What could it be? A wizard or a muggle?
I ran away as fast as I could,
I was too frightened to stay and struggle.

I opened my eyes and sat up very fast,
It was a nightmare, all in my head,
My mythical nightmare was over at last,
I was safe and sound in my comfortable bed.

Christie Jones (10)
Duns Primary School, Duns

A Starry Night

A peaceful scene,
A moonlit lake with a bright beam.
I walk around the lake so bright,
I walk a shimmering sight.

What is that I see?
I won't let my feelings overwhelm me.
Out of the mist came an elegant creature,
It's the most beautiful thing in the universe.

As it swiftly comes down to land,
Its outstretched wings look very grand.
I slowly bow to the majestic entity,
As it bows back, I am totally carefree.

Its horns glinting in the starry night,
Its eyes shining like a headlight.
Both our eyes met,
I know this is a dream I won't forget!

Dearbhla Gairnéir (11)
Gaelscoil An Chaistil, Ballycastle

Unicorns

In a dark, dark forest,
Lives a unicorn,
Crunch, crunch in the leaves,
She walked over to me,
There were fairies on her,
The fairies were singing, 'La la la la,'
The unicorns were multicoloured,
So were the fairies,
The fairies hopped off,
Boom, boom, boom,
The fairies took my hand,
They stopped singing,
They smelled like lavender,
All I could hear was still *crunch, crunch,*
They took me into a magical cave,
It looked like a chocolate house,
But I heard my mum's voice,
I woke up, it was only a dream.

Abbi McKinley (8)
Gaelscoil An Chaistil, Ballycastle

Dragons And Fairies

Pew, pew, pew!
A war went on,
Between the dragons and fairies,
They were all on a battlefield,
When the battle began.
They had lots of weapons like...
The dragons had armour,
Shields and swords,
The fairies had armour,
Machine guns and magic wands,
They raced into the middle of the field,
And started the war.
As it went on,
Less fairies than there used to be,
Their wings started to vanish,
They got stepped on by accident,
I was so scared until I woke up,
And realised it was all a dream...

Lucy Nic Conmara (10)
Gaelscoil An Chaistil, Ballycastle

Unicorn And Clown

Clowns are unicorns' worst enemies.
Clowns will creep up on you in the night,
Unicorns will bring you to the light!
And together they will have a battle.
Boom!
They will fight on the battlefield beside the clouds.

I feel very magical right now.
The unicorns made machine guns with their horns
And the clowns have baseball bats.

The unicorns will fight until all the clowns are dead,
But then the unicorns feel sorry for the clowns.
Then I wake up and it was just a dream.

Isla Goodlad (10)
Gaelscoil An Chaistil, Ballycastle

Final Kick

There wasn't long left,
And the crowd was crazy,
It looked like there was no success,
'One minute left,' said the referee.

The striker was coming,
As fast as lightning,
The crowd was roaring,
But I saved it, it was stunning!

I threw the ball to my striker,
He shoots like a cannonball,
The defender ducks
We win it all!

The team lifts the trophy
And we all celebrate!

Aaron Mac Pháil (10)
Gaelscoil An Chaistil, Ballycastle

Fairy Land

As deep as a volcano
A hole
I felt the warm breeze from below
Boom!
I fell right down
I looked around
Fairies and unicorns
Dancing around
Boom!
A flower lift
How did I get here?
I heard a voice
'Hello,' she said
The fairy queen
Now I'm in a magical cave
She pulled me into a waterfall
Swish!
As warm as the sun
Now I was a fairy.

Maebh Sands Robinson (9)
Gaelscoil An Chaistil, Ballycastle

Peacock The Dragon

I'm in a magical world,
There are dragons everywhere,
I want a ride,
There's one,
'Come here,' I called,
Whish, whish, whish, he came,
He let me up,
Feel the scaly back,
Whish goes the wind,
Smell the burnt fire,
'Roar,' you can hear,
See the sight,
Oh no,
I'm home,
The dragon,
I'll name him Peacock.

Aoife Kinney (9)
Gaelscoil An Chaistil, Ballycastle

The Fantastic Football Match

Five minutes to go
I'm running with the ball
I score, 1-0 to us.
From the kick-off they almost score
Luckily our keeper saves it
And it goes out for a corner
De Bryune takes it
And it goes in
Thirty seconds left!
My teammate running with the ball and gets fouled
It's a penalty!
And I'm taking it
I score
We win the match.

Críostpir ó Torráin (10)
Gaelscoil An Chaistil, Ballycastle

Barn Pig

B arn is red and big
A aron works in the barn with pigs every day
R ight away, every morning, Aaron feeds pigs
N ice barn with pigs big and small

P ig is nice and pink
I n the barn he stays at night
G reat little pig is the best in the world.

Reannán Meggitt (11)
Gaelscoil An Chaistil, Ballycastle

Fairies

Fairies flying in the bright sky
A wonderful castle
Lovely, sprightly fairies on a trip
In the dark, dark forest
Crunch, crunch, crunch
It was only a kind unicorn
Very fluffy
Smells beautiful
White as a wall
Took them to Rainbow Land
Oh, the unicorns are gorgeous.

Aileen Goodlad (8)
Gaelscoil An Chaistil, Ballycastle

Once Upon A Time

Phew! Phew! Phew!
The clowns are trying to shoot me!
The war has begun between the clowns and my army.
My army was strong, they trained every day and
every night.
In the end, my army won!
But...
Then I woke up,
It was all a dream.

Conán Mac Amhlaoibh (10)
Gaelscoil An Chaistil, Ballycastle

Hungry Wolves

I was in the forest.
There were wolves that were hungry.
They had rocket launchers!
I was scared.
They were trying to kill me.
I threw them off a cliff.
They landed on pillows.
They bounced back up.
Then they ate me.

Cónan Pearse Mac Fhirléighinn (9)
Gaelscoil An Chaistil, Ballycastle

My Family Is My Life

My mum, my dad, my baby bro.
They keep me safe, they keep me warm.
They keep me safe from harm.
My dad, he's big, he's strong, he's brave.
My mum, she's kind, she's loving, she's caring.
My bro, he's cute, he's funny, he's playful!
My dog, he's joyful, he's happy, he's springy!
In my dream I would take my family to space
To see the aliens and to float in the gravity
The aliens were grumpy, sometimes angry
and annoying
The little ones played football with dust
And talked really funny like goobly glob, ha ha ha.

Macauley Mateer Carson (10)
Malvern Primary School, Belfast

The Perfect Dream

I go to bed
To rest my head,
I close my eyes and close them tight
Because in my dream world it's such a delight.
Magical unicorns follow me everywhere.
With their mane so bright and so fair.

Happy pixies flying so high
With the magical sheep floating by.
With candyfloss clouds and bushes made of mint ice cream
It truly is the perfect dream.

Cheeky little dogs and cute little kitties
Playing with all the twinkly little pixies.
The rain is chocolate, so is the river.
But when you dive in you won't shiver.

Gingerbread houses with chocolate doors
And fluffy marshmallow floors.

And then I woke up, I knew it was a dream
But it was no ordinary dream, it was a perfect dream.

Jodie Sterritt (10)
Mullaglass Primary School, Newry

Candy Land

Me, in this rocket
As red as strawberries, so beautiful
But suddenly
It turned into an icing rocket!

We saw this fun-looking island
We landed the icing rocket, jumped out and landed on the island
That had a sign on it saying 'Candy Land'.

I saw these unicorns and other cute animals
My family were excited
To see what other things there were
To see.

We found this house
Made of cupcakes and hard chocolate.

My daddy and I went into the candy house
Went into the bedroom and didn't find beds
But found straw all over the floor
We went further and found a family of unicorns.

The unicorns could talk!
The mummy unicorn said, 'Hello, my name is Stardust, Where are you from?'

I said, 'I am from Earth, Northern Ireland.'

Bang! Suddenly, I woke up
It was morning time
Time to go to school
My mummy woke me up, it scared me
I really wanted to stay in my dream.

Emily Annett (10)
Mullaglass Primary School, Newry

Story Land

The flowers they were so bright,
As we flew through the night,
My unicorn lit up like a light,
Then little faces looked up to see,
Just my unicorn and me.

We landed in Story Land,
Then a little elf took my hand,
We were greeted by a band,
We walked into a great hall,
Where there was a ball.

With pixies dancing on a table top,
And a frog that could barely hop,
That's when one of the balloons went pop,
I was invited for some tea,
Where I saw the Princess and the Pea.

I hoped Prince Charming would dance,
Because he dances with so much romance,
And makes Bambi prance,
We went outside,
Where I saw the unicorn hide.

A big giant came towards me,
Then I was shocked to see,
That the giant was offering me a cup of tea,
Bang! I bumped my head,
On the side of my bed.

Grace Hamilton (10)
Mullaglass Primary School, Newry

Somewhere Over The Rainbow

I look around and all I can see,
Are cheeky little pixies dancing on a tree.
Their teeth are sparkling as white as snow,
And have rosy cheeks that glow and glow.

I turn around and it seems to be,
There's a magical unicorn smiling at me.
I wonder if all this is true,
There are so many wonderful things here to do.

The pixies invited me in for a lovely cup of tea,
The badgers come along and seemed happy
to meet me.
Rainbowdrop spoke and I said, 'Wow-ee,'
I wonder what pretty place he will take me to see.

So we flew in the air like a big balloon,
Oh what fun Rainbowdrop and I had under that
big silvery moon.
Suddenly, I lifted up my head,
And there I was in my old wooden bed.

Ellen Hamilton (10)
Mullaglass Primary School, Newry

The Big Red Clown

I was on holiday
In New York.
And I thought on one of the first nights
That I could go to see some sights.

I walked through the shopping centre
And I heard *bang! Bang! Bang!*
In the shadows, I saw a big red nose
As red as a rose.

Suddenly, it was a big clown!
I was as scared as a puppy would be
I ran as hard as I could,
Hoping he wouldn't use me for food.

I ran, ran and ran
Soon I woke up
I was confused, my heart wouldn't stop beating.
I heard a voice, I thought it was the clown
I hid under the covers
I then realised that it was my mother.

Emily Morrow (10)
Mullaglass Primary School, Newry

The Big Scary... Clown...

My parents left me at Tesco
I had to do the shopping
As they were away for the night
I would soon be home alone and I might get a fright.

I was walking back home,
So slowly like a tortoise,
When suddenly I was backed into a corner,
And fell into... dog poo!

I opened my eyes and looked up,
It was a clown, a very creepy clown,
I tried ringing my parents on my phone,
But, the clown snatched it off me and threw it, and it hit off a stone.

All I could see was a big red nose as red as a rose,
But I suddenly woke up to find myself in bed,
It was all a dream in my head.

Ruby Joanne McCartney (9)
Mullaglass Primary School, Newry

The Nightmare

I was going to the haunted house and I was by myself.
As I walked closer, two strange shadows appeared.
One was very small and the other one looked as if it had an afro.

I was petrified when I saw them.
I stood as still as a statue because they were walking towards me.
They got so close to me I could clearly see them now.

It was a leprechaun and a killer clown and
they were real.
I was as scared as having a spider crawling up
your back.
I then went into the haunted house before they could get me.

Beep, beep, beep!
I woke up with a fright
From the night.

Lois Boyd (10)
Mullaglass Primary School, Newry

Four Killer Clowns

I was going to meet my friends,
We were going bowling,
We were in a game,
Bang! The power went out,
We saw red eyes like a rose,
The power came on,
Jack said, 'Killer clowns!'

'Run to my house.'
'No,' Jack said,
'Call the police.'
The clowns ran away,
We're now at my house,
Ding dong!
The clowns are back,
What do we do?
Out the window,
A clown got me, 'Help!'
Ah! It's just a dream, is it?

Nathan Cartmill (10)
Mullaglass Primary School, Newry

Candy Land!

One night I went to sleep
On an adventure I did go
I visited a Candy Land
And with fizzy soda the river did flow.

A toffee dog pulled me
Towards a candy house
With a giant chocolate fountain
And a hall with not a mouse.

Then the gobstopper sun went down
And then a shiny silver wrapper moon
Came into the sky and
Soon people started to see the moon.

Then I shut my eyes and then opened them again
I found out I was back in my room.

Andrew McCartney (10)
Mullaglass Primary School, Newry

My Dream

I Sophie, could see the stars
I could see my old friend the BFG
We flew to Pluto
Met some dwarves and had tea.

We played some of their games
And some of our games, it was really nice
We rustled in the leaves,
And skated on the ice.

We had a game of dreams
And looked up into the skies
I fell asleep and was back in my bed
When I opened my eyes.

Melanie Wylie (11)
Mullaglass Primary School, Newry

Nursery School

T eacher for a nursery school
E veryone knows her to love
A dventure on the way, what will it bring?
C aught, what happened under my nose?
H er evil side, who knew what was inside!
E vil teacher trying to steal my place
R eally want to see what my dream will bring. *Beep beep beep!*

Zara Moffett (10)
Mullaglass Primary School, Newry

Candy Land!

C hocolate is everybody's friend
A nd cake is great
N obody is going to be sad
D ay by day you can stay
Y ou can eat all you want

L ove your food kids
A nd eat them up
N othing is going to go
D reaming of Candy Land.

Rachel Paul (11)
Mullaglass Primary School, Newry

Believe In Dreams

U nicorns are in my dream
N ight after night
I 'll never forget them
C lose your eyes
O pen your imagination and let it go wild
R un to the rainbow
N ever stop
S hare your dreams and believe, just like magic, because anything can happen.

Ellen Faloon (11)
Mullaglass Primary School, Newry

Football

F ootball is my dream
O n fields they play
O h how I wish to play with Chelsea
T oday is the day that I will play
B lack boots on the ready
A day at Stamford Bridge
L et's go Chelsea
L eap, leap, what? Oh, a dream.

Melissa Harshaw (11)
Mullaglass Primary School, Newry

The Big Mistake

I fall asleep
I drift away
From the clouds
I saw a frog leap
Another world, another sky
Oh, how I wish I could fly
The guard that keeps us safe
The black clouds overtake
The people make a run
To escape
But the people make a big mistake.

Yasmin Rose Muldrew (11)
Mullaglass Primary School, Newry

Never Mess With A Pokémon!

P ikachu electrocutes
O n Jupiter in my dreams
K ick, punch and a slap on the face
É nded with a *beep, beep, beep*
M orning sunshine
O n the planet Jupiter
N ever mess with a Pokémon.

Abbi Bradley (10)
Mullaglass Primary School, Newry

Dreams

D ancers dancing in the royal ball
R oyalty in Candyland
E lephants in the jungle
A thletes winning a gold medal
M onsters eating fairies
S pider-Man swings from city to city, watching the world go by.

Archie Alderdice (9)
Mullaglass Primary School, Newry

Friends Forever

F riends for life
R eal friends are true
I miss you so much
E rin will you ever come back?
N ever leave my sight
D ream, dream, dream, I wish this wasn't a dream.

Abbie Laura Nummy (11)
Mullaglass Primary School, Newry

Footballers And Dinosaurs

One day there was a football match.
The footballers were getting ready for the match.
They didn't know who they were playing.

They were playing dinosaurs!
They were giants.
They had big feet and big bodies.

They pushed the footballers about.
One almost broke their leg.
The dinosaur said, 'You are way too small.'

The dinosaurs scored and scored.
And tackled and tackled.
The footballers couldn't believe it.

Then the dinosaurs won, the footballers were frustrated.

Harley Muir (10)
Newbuildings Primary School, Londonderry

My Marvellous Dream

I opened my eyes,
And I fell from the sky.
Boing! I landed on a huge trampoline,
I bounced into the sky.
I saw candyfloss clouds,
And the sky was as brown as chocolate.
'Argh!' *Boom!* I was on the ground,
I saw a little house, it was as cute as candy.
I ran over to it,
'Hello little boy.'
'I thought houses couldn't talk.'
'Anything can happen in Dreamland.'
'Hey, why don't you come inside me?'
'OK.'
I went in.
So colourful!

Dylan Coyle (10)
Newbuildings Primary School, Londonderry

The Imaginary Man

There was a man who loved cars,
He dreamed he could go to Mars,
Once, he drove his car on a road,
Then he saw a portal,
He fell in it to another dimension,
Then he was a car!
He was surprised to be a car,
In a different dimension,
He slept in a big garage,
With a cosy bed.
The next day when he woke,
There was a twister!
The other cars drove away,
But the man stayed
The man got sucked up in the twister!
Luckily it was a dream. 'Phew!'

David Guy (9)
Newbuildings Primary School, Londonderry

Crazy Clown

Where are you crazy clown?
I saw you last night.
I just want you to know
You gave me such a fright.
Your crazy curls and squeaky nose.
When I saw you I just froze.
Why did you just stand there
And stare back at me?
It made me uneasy and woke me from my sleep.
So please crazy clown, just leave me alone
And don't come into my dream zone!

Jason McIvor (9)
Newbuildings Primary School, Londonderry

Dreams

D azzling stars in the sky
R eminds me of the time gone by
E very wish can come true
A ny wish for me and you
M y dreams are flying high
S o let's take it to the sky.

Samuel Wray (10)
Newbuildings Primary School, Londonderry

A Night Sky Gone By

When the sky goes dark and clouds disappear
All of a sudden, my dreams appear.

Feeling cosy in my bed
Lots of thoughts come to my head
I see pictures and I feel free
I can see a little girl, it is me.

Stars light up the sky
I feel like I can fly
The twinkle in my eyes shines so bright
My favourite time of day has to be night.

I fall into a deep restful sleep
Nothing can wake me not even a peep.

Remembering the fun times that make me laugh
I feel like I am sitting in a bubble bath
All white and fluffy like bouncy clouds
I feel so comfy and shout aloud,
'I'm so happy, I like it here'
I have no fears, they disappear.

Caitlin-Lea Hamilton (10)
Oakgrove Integrated Primary School, Londonderry

The Crazy Night-Time Dream

Time to go to bed, it is almost half past nine,
For school in the morning I'll be totally fine.
I jump into bed for my night-time kiss,
Well I love feeling so safe like this.
I dream I am flying through the air,
Zapping Voldemort with my wand so fair.
I start to sing on stage with Ariana Grande,
After that we go and have a good party.
We all sing our hearts out and have amazing fun,
Then I go and get a big chocolate bun.
I become an astronaut and fly to the moon,
It is almost time to go back home soon.
We go back home to go to bed,
I am sleeping and dreaming crazy things in my head.
'Wow!' I get up at quarter to three,
I still have lots and lots more to sleep!

Ajala Tench (10)
Oakgrove Integrated Primary School, Londonderry

Camogie Wish

The whistle blew and off I went
The cold air was raging by
My boots were gripping tight to the pitch
I soloed running fast
I avoided my opponents
Swaying left and turning right
I didn't tire, the goals were in sight
The clock was ticking, little time was left
Crowds were cheering at the top of their voices, encouraging me on
I struck the sliotar hard aiming for the goals
It went high and long, it was dropping to the crossbar
I was still running, following it, hoping it to go into the net
The crowd were happy, roaring and screaming
Where had the ball landed? I could not see!
Players had gathered, blocking the goals
The goalie had her back to me, she was all bent over
Goal! I had scored, I had scored!
I went running back out on the field being hugged by my teammates
The whistle blew, the game was over
We were all Ireland champions! All Ireland champions!

'Breakfast,' I heard Mum shout, 'are you getting up?'
Awwww, if only I was still in Croke Park!

Meabh Quinn (10)
Our Lady's & St Mochua's Primary School, Armagh

African Lions

A frican lions in the pride land
F ierce and frightening because they're so grand
R eally sharp teeth and roaring so loud
I 'm seriously scared now in case I'm found
C an't even breathe in case they give chase
A hunter's approaching to get himself an ace
N ever had I ever been so afraid

L ions are colossal and oh so, so brave
I n my tent I think I'm going to cave
O h my God! I need to pluck up courage
N ever again! I don't want to discourage
S wear, I'm safe and sound, they've all gone away

I'm so relieved I survived that crazy day!

Dáire Finn (9)
Our Lady's & St Mochua's Primary School, Armagh

Adventure

A t long last I awoke but all I could see was dense smoke
D own the hill and up the river, a rainforest appeared from nowhere
V iolets appeared, a monkey came and said its name was Jazz, what a surprise
E verlasting rivers came to a stop as I got a very big shock
N ature came, animals from near and far to join the fun
T umbling leaves flew into the air as we ran to the most exciting part yet
U nbelievable animals were there, like Carrie the cockatoo who always flew and Flo the flamingo with her long legs and neck, keeping everyone in check
R aindrops fell and parrots flew
E nd has come to our adventure as we glide back to soft pillows.

Clare O'Hare (10)
Our Lady's & St Mochua's Primary School, Armagh

Baby Sophie

Button eyes shining bright,
I could nurse her all night,
Baby Sophie, what a doll,
'Time for bottle,' I hear Mum call.

Rosy cheeks and black, black hair,
Her new blanket and teddy sat on the chair,
I hold her tight as she starts to wiggle,
She squirms and kicks and I start to giggle.

I think she looks like her daddy now,
But babies change every day somehow,
She puts a twinkle in my eye,
And a smile in my heart, I cannot lie.

She is so cute, my new baby cousin,
In my family there is now a dozen,
Sophie Ellen is her name,
I want to hold her again and again.

Jessie Carr (10)
Our Lady's & St Mochua's Primary School, Armagh

Not Another Nightmare!

When I go to sleep at night I can't sleep a wink.
Will I have a nightmare? Is all I seem to think.
When I close my eyes my greatest fears come to life.
I see creepy clowns sharpening a knife.
Even though I know it's fake.
I feel so nervous the ground starts to shake.
My friends have dreams about unicorns.
Flying around with shiny horns.
Oh, but me, never!
I hope my nightmares don't last forever.
When I tell people about my nightmares they never care.
Even though they give me such a scare.
I ask myself the question...
Will I have a nightmare tonight?
Or will I have another fight?

Sarah Renaghan (10)
Our Lady's & St Mochua's Primary School, Armagh

Candy Land

I glide off to sleep,
Then suddenly I'm there,
Through the candyfloss trees I peep,
To see a pink unicorn standing there!

The chocolate river flows,
And the lollipop flowers twirl,
I build a marshmallow snowman,
With a Haribo for a nose!

Suddenly, I feel twinkling on my hand,
It's raining sugar in this crazy land!
The sugar has now gone away,
But the blue sky will forever stay!

Now the land begins to fade,
My adventure for today is now made!
Don't worry, I will be back soon,
Because I always dream when I see the moon!

Emma Gaffney (10)
Our Lady's & St Mochua's Primary School, Armagh

When I Grow Up...

All I see is a track long and ever so wide.
I'm nervous and determined.
I look around, all I see for a minute is the sun.
I see my mum, dad and brothers.
They make me feel better.
Then I see the other racers.
I'm scared and for a moment I'm about to walk away.
I stop.
I remember all the days when I was training in the rain, the hail and even snow.
I turn back.
Bbbaaaannngg! The gun! I run!
After a moment I feel like the track goes on forever and ever.
Eventually, I get there coming first!
When I grow up this is what I'll do.

Caoimhe Hourican (10)
Our Lady's & St Mochua's Primary School, Armagh

The Temple Of Kahuna

My name is Alex,
I explore the land.
I search for gold,
Over hills and desert sand.

Monkey Man, my trusted friend,
Tags along until the end.
We wade through rivers,
Climb the trees,
The jungle vine and the seven seas.

Searching for gold,
Glittering and shimmering,
Feeling scared, but the excitement simmering.

At last we find the Temple Kahuna,
Only stopped by a large laguna.

Our future is here,
Monkey Man can cheer,
A life of Riley,
Awaits, my dear.

Alejandro Arroita (10)
Our Lady's & St Mochua's Primary School, Armagh

A Horse To Love

I ride the bus to school each day.
I pass the same horse on my way.
At times he's outdoors eating grass,
Beside a rail fence when I pass.
But when he's standing in his shed,
Then I just see his neck and head.
The horse is spotted grey on white.
His ears and mane and tail are light.
I'd like to take the horse a treat,
A carrot or some fruit to eat.
I'd like to pat his ears and nose,
And rub his neck. Do you suppose?
I'll have a horse when I grow up?
A spotted horse to love? My own?

Caitlin Rafferty (10)
Our Lady's & St Mochua's Primary School, Armagh

My Baking Dream

Since I was a little girl
I've seen my granny bake
I watch her very carefully
Ice her yummy cakes.

I dream of being a baker
Just like granny is
I love to eat her pastry
Let's hope mine is just as tasty
I'll bake for all occasions
Birthdays, weddings, Christmas and more.

Decorating is my favourite thing
Writing names and messages
Selling and sharing, giving people lots of cakes
Makes me want to bake and bake!

Aoife Drumm (10)
Our Lady's & St Mochua's Primary School, Armagh

Candyfloss

C louds of candy, I can't believe it
A couple of elves come my way
N ot one without a smile on their face
D ragons are flying around the sky
Y ou could say it's the perfect place to be
F illed with happiness and joy
L ots to do and see
O ver the edge I see not such a happy place
S ightseeing too far to the edge, I fall out
S uddenly, I wake up to find it was just a dream!

Orla Haughey (10)
Our Lady's & St Mochua's Primary School, Armagh

My Favourite Game

M y favourite hobby is playing this game
I can build and I have a good aim
N ever have I loved a game so much
E veryone says I have the magic touch
C reating my dream house, I love it so much
R ed stone is the material that builds so well
A ll my friends are so good at playing as well
F ree time is when I play my game
T omorrow I shall do it all again.

Stephen Mone (10)
Our Lady's & St Mochua's Primary School, Armagh

Sweets

Sweets, sweets, they melt in your mouth
They taste so nice you could scream and shout
All different colours like red, yellow and blue
Why don't you try them too!
Don't eat too much or the dentist will pout
And then your mum and dad will shout
You go to sleep at night and dream
All about a sweetie stream
So nice and flavoured too
Sweets to share among me and you!

Emma Gollogly (9)
Our Lady's & St Mochua's Primary School, Armagh

Super Teacher

S ome day in my classroom
U nder my wing
P laying and laughing
E njoying everything
R eading and writing

T imes tables to learn
E xpecting one day
A good wage to earn
C lassroom filled with laughter
H appiness not torture
E veryone having fun
R eaching for the future.

Seán óg McNaughton (10)
Our Lady's & St Mochua's Primary School, Armagh

Viva España

S unny beaches, blue skies every day
P aella, tapas and ice creams every way
A mazing slides in the water park
I ce-cold drinks served from morning to dark
N ever will forget the sunny isle, that always brings a big smile.

Shea Murray (10)
Our Lady's & St Mochua's Primary School, Armagh

Mrs Fairy Mouse

F lying in the sky
A ll alone at night
I see the stars shining
R olling through the clouds so bright
I nto the morning
E very second counts
S hanna is my name and I'm a fairy mouse.

Shanna McDermott (9)
Our Lady's & St Mochua's Primary School, Armagh

Dream

D reams, dreams, may come true
R emember, remember, it is just for you
E ating ice cream until it's gone
A ll have fun till it's dawn
M orning light shines so bright
S leep tight tonight.

Niamh Duffy (10)
Our Lady's & St Mochua's Primary School, Armagh

The Show Must Go On

I'm standing behind the curtain, trembling with fear, knowing the time is coming near.
Roslinn shouting, 'Good luck girls!' Dancing around with her shiny curls.
Grace decides to hold my hand and Sarah, fix my hair band.
I peek, my heart starts beating fast as I get a flashback from the past.
I am, I'd say, three years old, dancing and doing what I'm told.
Happy as Larry away I go until oh no, what do you know, the lights go off,
I fall off stage and get laughed at by big bully Paige.
I am really scared but, the show must go on!
The curtains open and in the front row is Simon Cowell, there to enjoy the show.
He enjoyed it very much and says, 'I have something to say...
You're all gonna be on Broadway!'

Ellie Fagan (11)
St Brigid's Primary School, Newry

Fairies And Berries

Once upon a dream, there were fairies that went to fetch some berries.
The fairies had to go and fetch some berries in the forest.
When the fairies had some berries other fairies came and took the berries.
I am with some fairies to catch some berries.
Some of the fairies are unhappy as all the other fairies took all the other berries.
The fairies needed more help to carry all the other berries that they'd found
So all the other fairies came and loaded all the other berries.

Hollie McCann (11)
St Brigid's Primary School, Newry

My New School

Oh, a new school
how scary
Moving to a new secondary
I'm on my way to class
all the new faces I pass
I wonder if the teachers are nice
Or if the dinners are at a high price.

I love home economics
and all the topics
This school is amazing
everyone's blazing
I told my mum and dad about
such a delight
They thought I would've shouted
With all my might.

Amy McMahon (10)
St Brigid's Primary School, Newry

The Winning Point

My biggest dream ever is to play for Down,
And here I am captaining the Down Team,
Playing in the All-Ireland final,
Going to kick the winning point.

The nerves are really starting to kick in now,
As I start to move towards the ball,
All the pressure is on me,
I am eager to sail the ball between the posts.

My heart is racing and my legs feel like jelly,
So I close my eyes after a quick look at the posts,
And I slice the ball and hope for the best!
I look up as anxious as ever, hoping to hear the roars.

But all of a sudden there was a *bang!*
The ball has hit the post!
But I see that I had hit the inside of the post,
And that I had split the posts!
My dream has finally come true,
I get to walk up the steps of the Hogan Stand,
To lift the Sam Maguire Cup!

James Keenan (11)
St Colman's Primary School & All Saints' Nursery Unit, Banbridge

My Adventure

I'm climbing a mountain
That's one thousand feet tall,
I'm being quite cautious
In case I slip and fall!

I'm a bit silly
I lost the grip of my friend,
He fell down and cut his leg
But that'll be easy to mend.

So we went on with our day
So far it's going good,
But there is a problem
We're seriously lacking in food!

We got some food
Deer was our menu,
We went to sleep because the sun went down, that was our cue.

In the morning,
I was packing all the food,
Then I slipped and fell,
That can't be good!

In mid-air,
I closed my eyes,
In a few seconds
I'm going to die!

3, 2, 1... *Boom!*
I've opened my eyes,
I'm in my bedroom, awake
I haven't died!

Cormac McNally (11)
St Colman's Primary School & All Saints' Nursery Unit, Banbridge

Feeling Free In A Wonderful Dream!

One sunny day down by the stream,
Watching the stream flow.
I got a breeze on my back while lying on the grass,
Whoosh! I'm freezing!
I grabbed my scarf and my bag filled with
Delicious sweets and treats,
For me, my mum and sister to eat.

There I go heading up the sunflower meadow,
I stopped for a rest under a tree until I realised
What was right behind me.
There it was, an old rusty swing,
Which I knew I didn't want to leave.

After all I had all the time I needed,
With me and the swing,
I knew I would remember the moments with glee!

I then decided to head off down the valley,
Until I saw a happy little grey bunny,
Who was also full with glee,
And then him and me relaxed under the
Little tree on the swing feeling free.

Clara Sheppard (10)
St Colman's Primary School & All Saints' Nursery Unit, Banbridge

Nothing Is Bland In Candyland

I went to bed and fell asleep,
In my cosy little bed,
Then all of a sudden,
There's a bright light
And I'm standing here in Candyland!

I feel as happy as Larry,
Glancing all around me, left, right and centre,
I can see people as pink as a pig,
I can see an old-looking man with a top hat and a stick,
And he takes my hand and pulls me along,
To a place that he calls home.

He takes me to a towering castle,
Made entirely out of clouds,
And offers me something extraordinary;
A fancy piece of floating rainbow!

I pick it up and try to eat it,
But I can't taste a thing,
Then suddenly everything fades away,
And unfortunately I find,
I'm back in bed, eating my pillow,
I realise it was just a dream!

Líle McArdle (11)
St Colman's Primary School & All Saints' Nursery Unit, Banbridge

The Nightmare For Me

I was sitting on a bench in my local park,
I was along with my friend Molly,
It suddenly got dark and windy,
I felt anxious, scared and upset!

I was suddenly surrounded by snakes, rats and spiders,
The snakes were scaly, the rats looked hairy and ugly,
And the spiders looked horrific,
Oh! It was so, so creepy!
As we sat there, to our dismay these terrible creatures
Thought we were their prey!
They began to scrape and scrabble and bite,
No, no, no, such a fright!

Boom! The next thing I knew I opened my eyes
And as I looked around I felt thrilled and surprised,
No nasty snakes, spiders or rats,
I was safe in my bed, thank goodness for that!

Aoibheann Elizabeth Heenan (10)
St Colman's Primary School & All Saints' Nursery Unit, Banbridge

My Own Magical Land

I sneak away into a magical land,
I can call my own,
Full of sweets for me to eat.
Where I can keep my secrets, fears and also regrets.

In an enchanted land,
Where I can be myself.
I go alone to my secret place,
Never leaving a trace.
Free like a bird in the sky,
No need to be shy.

I lie back,
While the warmth of the sun,
Blazes through the trees onto my face,
I can only compare it to my mother's embrace.

My enchanted land is full of fairies,
I can speak to.
Oh my gosh, I feel so much like Snow White.

Whoosh! Bang! Thump!
Why do I have to wake,
From this dream full of delight.

Kyra Haughey (11)
St Colman's Primary School & All Saints' Nursery Unit, Banbridge

Hug Me Tight And Say Goodnight!

I'm in this town called Worque Ranks,
Jack and I see a sign for planks.
There is a weird-shaped house,
And weirdly stacked floors.

We walk in and *bang!* A cage dropped on us,
We are split up, but why?
We yelled goodbye,
As we jumped up high.

We did challenges to escape,
I felt strange and scared,
I didn't quite care,
Until I heard sounds.

There I saw monsters and killer clowns,
I didn't like it so I didn't do it,
I closed my eyes,
And opened them.

By surprise,
I'm in my bed,
So warm and safe,
So I stayed in bed.

Kate O'Rourke (11)
St Colman's Primary School & All Saints' Nursery Unit, Banbridge

The Nightmare I Wasn't Prepared For

I drift off to sleep,
My mum kisses me goodnight,
But nothing has prepared for this,
In the night I usually get a fright,
A lot of fun rides around me,
But in the distance a frowning tree,
So I go over to it,
There is a door on it,
I say, 'Ouch! You bit me.'
But it just stood there and gave a nice little grin,
I opened the tiny little door,

I see a crying girl in the corner,
I go over to her and say,
'Are you okay?'
So she turned around and said,
'Sweet dreams,' with a knife in her hand,
One, two, three, *boom!*
I won't come back too soon.

Killian Sean Loughlin (10)
St Colman's Primary School & All Saints' Nursery Unit, Banbridge

My Dream Car

On Saturday night I fell asleep on the chair
I could see my car, it was all done up
My dad got the Peugeot for my birthday, I loved it.

Oh, but the best thing of all,
My dad and myself we headed for the town
We got her all spruced up, tinted windows, fancy alloys,
You name it, we got it with a few pounds out of the bank.

Then I dreamt that there was rockets on my car
And it flew down the road and then into the sky
And next down to the ground with a bump.

Then suddenly, I woke up in my room
It was a dream
I thought it was real but it was actually not.

Darragh Greenan (11)
St Colman's Primary School & All Saints' Nursery Unit, Banbridge

Candyland

I went and woke up in Candyland,
I was very excited to wake up here,
I was wondering where everyone was,
I started to explore, I became very scared.

I landed with a thump and a sphere house appeared,
There was a chocolate mouse,
It was at a farm,
And I set off the popcorn alarm!

The cows are made out of chocolate,
The sheep are like fluffy marshmallows,
A man came out and his name is Gary,
He made a house with his friend Barry.

I woke up from my dream,
I found a plate of sweets,
I ate them all and said,
'Oh, what a lovely time I had!'

Oisin McAvoy (11)
St Colman's Primary School & All Saints' Nursery Unit, Banbridge

Fright Night

Finally bed, the place I want to be.
I saw a scary movie I shouldn't have seen.
I dive into bed and tuck under the covers,
I just want to get this night over.
My mum comes in and kisses me goodnight.
The lights go off, and suddenly I'm fast asleep...

I wake up, lying flat on the floor.
This is not my bedroom and there's no door.
It's very misty and I can barely see,
Back in the distance, I see eyes glaring at me.

I decide to walk on,
Towards the creepy that are shining very bright.
Those eyes are looking very angry and giving me a fright.

Paul Heenan (11)
St Colman's Primary School & All Saints' Nursery Unit, Banbridge

The Future Car

I will go buy it for £450,
The man said, 'That is alright'
Before I hand him the money I'll take it for a test drive,
It's a great sight.

The car is a Peugeot 306,
When I take it for a drive I hope it is as fast as a rocket
And it will win top prize.

I got my dad to drive it home,
It was very fast,
I can't wait till I get on the phone,
I will insure and bring it to the scrapyard.

When I have the money,
I know exactly what to do,
I'll put fuel in my aeroplane,
And take the whole school to see Man U.

Aaron McKay (11)
St Colman's Primary School & All Saints' Nursery Unit, Banbridge

The Royal Circus

I went to bed,
And fell fast asleep.
Soon I found myself beside the Queen,
Dancing monkeys and happy hippos is what I'd seen.

My mummy, my dog Jimbo and I,
Are as lucky as could be.
When the monkey jumped in front of me,
It gave me an enormous fright,
While Jimbo gave a little bile!

My mummy was delighted to see,
The animals entertained me.
Then I turned and smiled,
For all the excitement I had for a while.

Soon I woke,
To a cup of tea.
I was back to reality,
It brought a tear to my eye,
But I did not cry.

Carla Quinn (11)
St Colman's Primary School & All Saints' Nursery Unit, Banbridge

Everest

It is dark and gloomy
Where I am is unknown
I am frightened and unnerved
I am not alone.

Trees and mountaintops as far as I can see
A silver bullet in the sky flowers
Where am I? Where could I be?
I am not alone.

Underfoot is slippy like walking on ice
A strong smell of wood to taste
Can I awake from this nightmare back to paradise?
I am not alone.

I hear them, they are coming
Running faster and faster, please someone help
Suddenly, quietness, the silence is numbing,
In bed at last, no longer afraid
I am alone.

Madison Greenan (11)
St Colman's Primary School & All Saints' Nursery Unit, Banbridge

Lost In Dream Land

I was going to bed,
I was a very sleepy head.
I looked out the window and saw some sleet,
Next I fell off my feet.

I started to dream,
Some dreams can be big.
Some dreams can be small,
And some dreams can be nothing at all.

I was flying my kite,
Then I got a big fright.
Because it was a bite,
Next I caught sight
Of a killer clown,
With a scowling chainsaw and a frown.

With the fright of the clown I woke up,
There was a cup
Of warm delicious tea,
And it was all for me.

Ruairí McAvoy (11)
St Colman's Primary School & All Saints' Nursery Unit, Banbridge

The Big Apple

I am standing beside the road,
All I can hear is screeching cars,
Lots of people are everywhere.
Then I realise my friend was beside me,
I look around and see the big sign 'New York'.

I can see the awesome Central Park,
I don't know what to do first,
I think I might go to the Empire State Building.
It's so big and interesting inside,
My friend would rather go somewhere else.

It's so much fun,
But wait, I find,
Myself in my own bed,
It was all a big dream.

Aoife McArdle (11)
St Colman's Primary School & All Saints' Nursery Unit, Banbridge

The Forest Flame

When I walk into the forest
I feel a slight breeze,
As something whizzes past me
And flies deep into the trees.

I'm not too sure what it was
But that's what made me so intrigued
To figure out what's lurking in the black fringe
of the forest.

I wander deeper, not knowing what I'm about to find.
I get closer and closer and see a glorious sight!
Not realising that there was a dragon behind me the
whole entire time.

From where I was standing I could see them all.
1, 2, 3, 4, 5 and millions more galore!
The fire-breathing beauties snuggling with their young!

I'm entranced by their beauty
And then feel a nudge as something lifts me
onto its back.
I can't bear to look but when I do,
The sky meets my gaze and I'm flying too!

On a dragon's back, soaring happily.
My eyes start fluttering and I know I have to leave.
I find the dragon swooping down, sensing I have to go.
I give him a hug and say I'll be back, and then he disappears
Out of sight!

I wake up grinning,
Telling everyone about my dream.
They think it's just my imagination
But I know it was real.

I rest my head on my pillow,
Can't wait to let the magic happen!
I drift into a deep sleep and find I'm in a forest
And there's the dragon waiting,
waiting for another adventure.

Niamh Orna Cunning (11)
St Columba's Primary School, Kilrea

The Royal Dream

I drowsily climb out of bed,
Taking in the floral bed sheets and beige curtains.
This is not my room.
Where am I?

I look into the gold-framed mirror and scream
At the reflection staring back at me.
I am Queen Elizabeth.
This can't be right.

There is a knock on the door.
A servant crossed the threshold.
'The President is waiting Madam.'
He leads me downstairs
And asks me to enter the room.

I gracefully enter.
Standing in front of me is a 6'3" monster.
It's got the head of a man,
The chest of an alligator,
The arms of a chicken
And the legs of a bear.
'Hi, I'm Donald,' it says to me.
Suddenly, I'm whisked away.

I open my eyes to find myself in my room.
Home sweet home.

Cághla Bradley (11)
St Columba's Primary School, Kilrea

My Nightmare

All I can see are my enemies,
Dinosaurs, clowns and evil fairies.
Some people are afraid and filled with fright
Here in the darkness of the night.

When they strike, everyone quivers.
When they hit, we start to shiver.
We are down, we hit the ground.
Some people laugh, some people frown.
Our team has lost the final round.

I see the builders and teachers with superpowers,
Walk into the woods with the bloodsucking vampires.
Everyone shrieks in despair, then they come out with no hair.

I run home with my friends.
Around the creepy monstrous bends.
We all see the creepy gloomy ghouls.
Submerge into their graves never to be seen again.
Or maybe they will come into your dreams and give you a fright
Tonight!

Fearghal O'Kane (11)
St Columba's Primary School, Kilrea

Land Of Sweets

I got into my bed and closed my eyes
And I woke up and saw houses made out of pies
Then I saw a unicorn with a rainbow mane
It said, 'Hello, do you want a candy cane?'
I said, 'Hello, what is your name, unicorn?'
'My name is Luna,' said the thing with a horn
Then my wonderful dream came true
I became president, and I didn't have a clue!
It was an absolutely lovely dream
Since my house was made of cream!

Clodagh Burke (10)
St Patrick's Primary School Legamaddy, Downpatrick

Nerf War

N ever had such Nerf armies gathered
E ven at the battle of Nerf Castle
R eally only rivalled King Nerf's army
F or the clouds of a Nerf war were brewing

W hen the armies charged only carnage was left in their wake
A nd they fought till the Taliban surrendered
R ight after that, the Taliban forces surrendered in all parts of Iraq.

John McLaughlin (11)
St Patrick's Primary School Legamaddy, Downpatrick

The Ulster Champion

I was soaring through the air
The adrenaline hit me
I was not easing off the throttle at all
Going through the corners
The sand was as soft as a blanket
I was slowly but surely moving up the positions
As fast as Usain Bolt
My bike was squealing
It couldn't go faster
The sand was flicking up in the air
And before I knew it
I was the Ulster Champion.

Ben Cope (11)
St Patrick's Primary School Legamaddy, Downpatrick

Once In A Lifetime Dream

Once upon a dream is where I want to be,
Where you can be anyone you wish,
Even something funny like a cow or fish!
You can dream of being a dancer and dance any style,
Or a famous football player who can run more than a mile!
You could be a singer or an actor too and win an Oscar all for you!
You could be something crazy like a wizard or kangaroo,
A lion tamer or secret spy,
But remember you are you!
So a teacher or doctor or even a queen maybe.
When you wake up you will know you are living in reality.
You are anything you dream to be, so don't give up on your,
Once in a lifetime opportunity!

Terri Devlin (10)
St Teresa's Primary School, Craigavon

Table Tennis

Ping, pong, ping, pong
The ball is as loud as Donkey Kong,
Although most people want to see,
We move from right to left,
And laugh and cheer at times I am hit
And landing in the net.
It is hard for men to understand,
That hurting me a lot,
Is hurting me so terrible,
And giving me blue spots,
But finally, when victory's there,
For one table tennis player,
He will be rewarded by his friends,
And also by the mayor.
They then caress me and I am kissed,
As if I am a little pup;
For despite my pain, they have won with me,
I have won the table tennis cup.

Aedan McGivern (9)
St Teresa's Primary School, Craigavon

Me And Cristiano Ronaldo

I turn my lamp off to go to bed
Then I see a theme park in my head
I look left, I look right
Then I see Ronaldo in my sight
He gives me popcorn and a kiss
Then I tick my bucket list
Suddenly, the light flashed before my eyes
I saw a new ride to my surprise
It was called the Terminator Three
Then I shouted out with glee
I went over to check it out
Then I give Ronaldo a shout
Me and him went on excited
Then Ronaldo threw up!
It was the best dream of my life.

Emily Mulgrew (10)
St Teresa's Primary School, Craigavon

The Swimming Pool Gala

Well, I'm here at Lurgan swimming pool,
These sixteen-year-olds think they're so cool.
Back crawl is the best!
But am I ready to put it to the test?
All around I see water,
Wow! That swimmer looks like she has daughters!
Ah! Was that the whistle blow?
I really need to go!
I'm in the water doing my task,
These sixteen-year-olds are so fast!
Phew! I'm glad that's done,
Wait, I think I won!

Sophie-Rose Henderson (9)
St Teresa's Primary School, Craigavon

The Waterfall

W here am I?
A m I dreaming or is this real?
T he way of the water makes me feel
E xhausted and relaxed
R eally? Where am I?
F alling through the air while some water splashes in my eye
A blood-curdling scream comes from my mouth
L ike a screaming mouse
L ovely relaxing bed, I'm happy that I'm awake.

Ben Whyte (10)
St Teresa's Primary School, Craigavon

My Midnight Garden

When I fall asleep I keep on having the same dream,
I dream of a living garden,
It's magical and amazing,
It smells of sweet sugar,
The clouds are candyfloss,
The stars are small people,
The grass is green Haribos, but yet,
The ground is a soft pillow,
The unicorns are everywhere and I'm a fairy!
I love this land and it loves me.

Martha Walsh (9)
St Teresa's Primary School, Craigavon

Through The Clouds

Running along the fluffy clouds in the sky,
With Tinky the fairy by my side.
The sun is smiling in our faces,
As we run through these magical places.
Sparkles the unicorn is at the top of the road,
So we spread our wings to go, go go!
Flying along to the castle ahead,
Then I wake up to find I'm still at home in bed.

Ella Forker (10)
St Teresa's Primary School, Craigavon

A Football Poem

I play football with my friends,
It's great fun with goals at both ends.
Attack, defence, headers and volleys,
No matter who wins, it's always a jolly.

My favourite player is Lallana,
Number 20, and his skills are so cool.
He plays for the mighty Liverpool.

Kieran Livingstone (10)
St Teresa's Primary School, Craigavon

Sadness

I don't know how to tell you I'm broken without feeling needy.
I don't know how to open up without feeling jumbled.
I don't know how to cry when my tears feel like fire.
I just need you to see that I'm hurting without me telling you.

Amani Gallagher (10)
St Teresa's Primary School, Craigavon

My Magic Dream

What is that up there in the sky, is it a fairy?
What if it's scary?
It looks very hairy.
I hope its name is Mary.

What is that? It sounds like a band.
Is it coming from Fairyland?
What are those at the front of the line, are they unicorns?
Are they throwing corn?

There is a whimpering wizard.
It is carrying a lizard.
Is that a wand?
Is it in a pond?

I am getting scared.
As scared as a bird when it first flies.
When can I go home
To my perfect little dome?

Georgia Rosenfeld (7)
Torphichen Primary School, Bathgate

An Awesome Dream About Technology In A School

My dream is about technology.
The school called psychology.
The probes have robes.
The probes go *bleep, bloop, blap!*

It took 5 years to build the floating neon tunnels which tinkle.
There is a cool pool in the school.
I said I had fun at lunch eating a bun.
The probes go *bleep, bloop, blap!*

I say I like it so let's bike it!
The probes have bikes from a garage called Nikes!
I have fun in the sun eating a bun.
I have a tonne.
The probes go *bleep, bloop, blap!*

Oskar de Joode (7)
Torphichen Primary School, Bathgate

My Ninjago Dream

My dream was about a Nindroid.
My dream was about Ninjago.
My dream was about four ninjas and a Samurai X.

Zane was a powerful, pro, pink Nindroid.
Zane was a white, weird, waddling ninja.
Zane was a walking, weird, writing Nindroid.
Zane was an awesome, amazing, aching ninja.

I was as inspired as an author reading another author's book.
I was as happy as a clown.
I was as impressed as a person looking at an artist's work.
I was so happy that my head was about to explode.

Ewan Samper (7)
Torphichen Primary School, Bathgate

Stuck In A Dream

In my dream the sun will beam.
In my dream I eat ice cream.
In my dream I seem to gleam.
In my dream I sit down by the stream.

The stream is sparkly.
The stream is shimmery.
The stream is shiny.
The stream is glimmery.

I am as happy as the happiest hippo.
I am as happy as the happiest hippo bathing in mud.
I am as happy as the happiest hippo bathing in mud by the pool.
I am as happy as the happiest hippo bathing in mud by the pool eating ice cream.

Laura Zoe Taylor (7)
Torphichen Primary School, Bathgate

My Adventure

My dream was about a castle.
My dream was about a wand.
My dream was about a wizard.
My dream was about a blizzard.

I feel as scared as a lost child.
I feel as nervous as an African child.
I feel as petrified as a lost puppy.
I feel as terrified as a lost cat.

I look at a clover.
I look up and over.
I look up and down.
I look all around.

I see a humongous tree.
I see a terrific tent.
I see a bent pole.
I see a big dent.

Charlotte Conchie (7)
Torphichen Primary School, Bathgate

The World Of The Sky

My dream was about me flying.
My dream was about no one dying.
My dream was about the sky.
My dream was about being able to fly.

When I was in the sky, I thought it must be a lie.
When I was in the air, I could see big brown bears.
When I was soaring over, I dashed straight past clover.
When I glided through trees, I struck past a nest of bees.

As I soared over the sea, I felt as happy as can be.
As I soared over the flowers, I felt happy for hours.

Rosie Kao (7)
Torphichen Primary School, Bathgate

My Beast Dream

My dream was about beasts.
My dream was about feasts.
My dream was about castles.
My dream was about battling.

Beasts who love balls.
Beasts who love other beasts.
Beasts who love drinking a bowl of soup.
Beasts who love Brussels sprouts.

The beast was as scary as a lion.
The castle was as epic as Cluedo.
The feast was as awesome as hangman.
I was as scary as a dragon.

Joe MacIver (7)
Torphichen Primary School, Bathgate

Tom's Dragons

My dream was about a dragon.
My dream was weird.
My dream was about dragons.
My dream was in a field.

I saw a big dragon.
I sit with a big dragon.
I cuddle a big dragon.
I love big dragons.

I live with dragons.
I marry dragons.
I think they're good dragons.
I really like dragons.

I love playing on my bike.
I like cake.
I like home.

Tom McFarlane (7)
Torphichen Primary School, Bathgate

My Football Dream

My dream was about a hall
My dream was about a football
My dream was about a brick
My dream was about Nick

My dream was super
My dream was cool
My dream was fun
My dream was exciting

I was playing fantastic football
I was playing in a huge hall
I was playing with my friends
I was playing well.

Cameron Fisher (7)
Torphichen Primary School, Bathgate

My Poem

My dream was about a plane.
My dream was fun.
My dream was good.
My dream was happy.

The plane was fun.
The plane was good.
The plane was epic.
The plane was cool.

I was as happy as a monkey.
I was as happy as a friend.
I was as happy as a family.
I was as happy as an angel.

Merryn Binnie (7)
Torphichen Primary School, Bathgate

My Dream

My dream was about sour sweets.
My dream was about small sweets.
My dream had some gummies.
My dream had some dummies.

I felt as happy as a baby getting candy.
I felt as clappy as a little girl seeing a unicorn.
I felt as excited as a little kid getting out of school.
I felt as excellent as a baby monkey.

Nethuki Nuthara Perera (8)
Torphichen Primary School, Bathgate

My Dream Poem

My dream was about a wizard.
My dream was scary.
My dream was about a wizard.
My dream was in a blizzard.

The wizard was Hairy.
The wizard was scary.
The wizard was freaky.

I was scared.
I was excited.
I wish this didn't happen.
I wish the wizard gone.

Alexander Neave (7)
Torphichen Primary School, Bathgate

My Dream

My dream was about a wizard.
My dream was in a blizzard.
My dream was with a wizard.
My dream was with a river.

My dream was about Hogwarts.
My dream was with Harry Potter.
My dream was with Hedwig.
My dream was with Hermione.

Fin Venters (7)
Torphichen Primary School, Bathgate

YoungWriters
Est.1991

YOUNG WRITERS INFORMATION

We hope you have enjoyed reading this book – and that you will continue to in the coming years.

If you're a young writer who enjoys reading and creative writing, or the parent of an enthusiastic poet or story writer, do visit our website **www.youngwriters.co.uk**. Here you will find free competitions, workshops and games, as well as recommended reads, a poetry glossary and our blog.

If you would like to order further copies of this book, or any of our other titles, then please give us a call or visit **www.youngwriters.co.uk**.

Young Writers
Remus House
Coltsfoot Drive
Peterborough
PE2 9BF
(01733) 890066
info@youngwriters.co.uk